This book is dedicated to my grandbabies George III, Grayson, Karoline, London, Lauren, Isiah and Nevy.

I hope this book inspires our future generation to do the best they can to make the world a better place to live in. The environment and climate control are huge concerns and the more we treat our earth with respect, the more the environment and climate will respect us.

A special thanks to my husband Allray Ben for being so loving, supportive, understanding, and the wind beneath my wings.

To my children Kelsi and George Beverly, Anthony Darty, Allison Ben, and Charity Ben. Believe that the impossible can become possible and use your highest form of research - your imagination.

To my loving mother, Mary Johnson, who is and has been my cheerleader in everything I do, thank you. To my daddy, rock, mentor, and a daughter's first love Harold Johnson, thank you for showing me that anything is achievable.

Queenie, What Do the Numbers Mean in the Recycling Triangle?

Written by:
Daphne Len Ben

Illustrated by:

105 PUBLISHING EST. 2020

"Queenie, I had so much fun learning how to recycle in the last book. Now my brother, sister, and I have less garbage and more recycling!"
"That is awesome!" Queenie said. "How do you feel Grayson?"

"I feel great, but I am curious, what do the numbers mean in the recycling triangle?"

"What a great question." Queenie replied. "Most people don't know what the numbers mean. On the bottom of most recyclable items, you will find a small number inside the recycling logo, which means the type of plastic/materials the containers are made from."

"Oh wow!" Grayson said.
"Remember how I told you that you are unique? So are recyclable items! They have special numbers on them that show us how to use them correctly. This is important to know so we can be safe with anything that we are recycling."

"Grayson, do you know what the colors on the traffic light mean?"
"Of course! Red = stop, yellow = slow down, and green = go!"

"Good job! The numbers in green let us know that it is a safe plastic/material to recycle. Yellow means to be cautious or like you said, slow down! Red is to stop or avoid. Stay clear of these, Grayson. Only adults should take care of this."

TYPES OF PLASTICS
and how recyclable they are

SYMBOLS

1 PET Polythylene Terephthalate	**2** HDPE High-Density Tolyethylene	**3** PVC Polyvinyle Chloride	**4** LDPE Low-Density Tolyethylene	**5** PP Plypropylene	**6** PS Polystyrene	 **7** PC Other

RECYCLABILITY (Check Locally)

Commonly Recyclable	Sometimes Recyclable	Not-Often Recyclable	Sometimes Recyclable	Sometimes Recyclable	Rarely Recyclable	Rarely Recyclable

EXAMPLES

 Safest Choice   Use With Caution   Avoid

"Just like when mommy tells me to stay away from the stove! Another question...why does the number system stop at 7?"

"Grayson, just by you sharing this information with others, you are helping to save the world. The more you share with others, the more we can learn and connect with each other. "

"Wow, Queenie! I can't wait to tell my friends at school!"

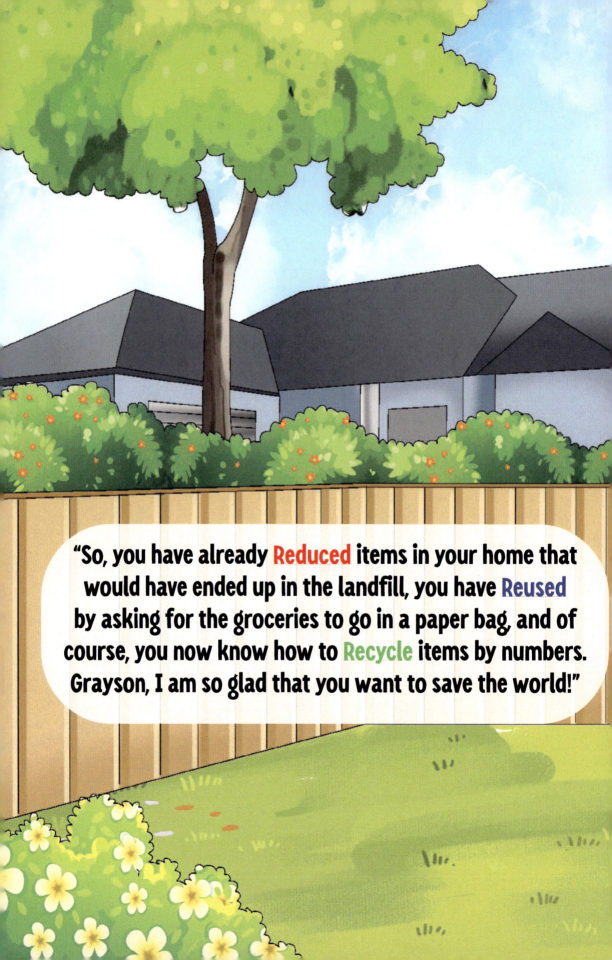

"So, you have already Reduced items in your home that would have ended up in the landfill, you have Reused by asking for the groceries to go in a paper bag, and of course, you now know how to Recycle items by numbers. Grayson, I am so glad that you want to save the world!"

THE END!

Next Books By Daphne Ben Aka Queenie:

- Book #3 Queenie explains the difference between recycling and compostable

- Book #4 Queenie explains how we can live off the earth

See the products you can recycle on the next pages!

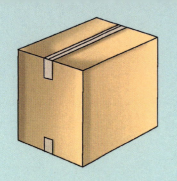

Shipping boxes

Newspapers and magazines

Plastic cups

Wrapping paper

Envelopes

Paperbags

Take out boxes

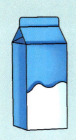

Milk and juice cartons

Paper

Pizza boxes

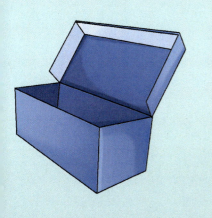

Shoe boxes

This is the 2nd book of a 4-book series!

http://booksbydaphnelenben.square.site
Books by Daphne Len Ben/Facebook page
Amazon
Barnes and Noble
Google Play Books

About the Author

Daphne Len Ben, AKA Queenie, was born on September 27, 1964 in Detroit, Michigan. She lived there until the age of 11 when her family transferred to Kalamazoo, Michigan in 1975. She is a graduate of Loy Norrix High School in 1982. Queenie received two master's degrees in Healthcare Administration and in Business Administration with a specialty in Human Resource Management. She has a bachelor's degree in Applied Science, is licensed as a Respecting Choice Facilitator, and is a Health Insurance Specialist. Queenie recently retired from Bronson Hospital after 40 years of dedicated service in various positions. She is a patient advocate, striving for change and justice. She is currently studying to be a Certified Holistic Nutritionist.

Queenie is a breast cancer survivor and educator, owner and operator of Queenie's Vegan Dog Food-n-Treats (http://queenies-vegan-dog-food-n-treats.square.site), a master gardener, and an aspiring artist. She is a grandmother of seven, mother of four, and loving wife to Allray Ben. Queenie believes that sharing knowledge with everyone encourages, enables, and empowers people to grow beyond their imagination. Children are our future. We must inspire, support, and allow them to be themselves. It is important to let children learn about all cultures to understand differences and similarities. Now let's go save the world!

105 Publishing LLC
Austin, TX
www.105publishing.com

14847059R00020